Masks

Helen and Peter McNiven

For Sophie

With photographs by Chris Fairclough

Wayland

FIRST ARTS & CRAFTS

This series of books aims to introduce children to as wide a range of media approaches, techniques and equipment as possible, and to extend these experiences into ideas for further development. The National Curriculum proposals for art at Key Stage One place particular emphasis on the appreciation of art in a variety of styles from different cultures and times throughout history. The series broadly covers the National Curriculum attainment targets 1) Investigating and Making and 2) Knowledge and Understanding, but recognizes that circumstances and facilities can vary hugely. Children should experiment with, and add to, all the ideas in these books, working from imagination and observation. They should also work with others, where possible, in groups and as a class. You will find suggestions for and comments about particular sections of work in the Notes for parents/teachers at the end of the book. They are by no means prescriptive and can be added to and adapted. Unless a particular type of paint or glue is specified, any type can be used. Aprons and old newspapers provide protection for clothes and surfaces when working with papier mâché, glue, paints etc. Above all, the most important thing is that children enjoy art in every sense of the word. Have fun!

Titles in this series
Collage, Drawing, Masks, Models, Painting, Printing, Puppets, Toys and Games

First published in 1994
by Wayland (Publishers) Ltd, 61 Western Road, Hove
East Sussex BN3 1JD, England
© Copyright 1994 Wayland (Publishers) Ltd
Series planned and produced by The Square Book Company

British Library Cataloguing in Publication Data
McNiven, Helen
Masks - (First Arts & Crafts Series)
I. Title II. McNiven, Peter III. Series
646.478
ISBN 0 7502 1013 3

Photographs by Chris Fairclough
Designed by Howland ■ Northover
Edited by Katrina Maitland Smith
Printed and bound in Italy by G. Canale & C.S.p.A., Turin

Contents

Making masks

A mask is another face for you to hide behind. You can become someone or something different. It makes you very mysterious.

People have made masks throughout history. Cave people wore masks to help them feel brave when they went out to hunt. The ancient Egyptians and many other peoples believed masks could protect them from evil.

Tassili rock painting, Algeria.

Kenyan tribal mask.

Actors have used masks to make them look like other people. This began in Greek and Roman times. Then people started wearing masks at festivals and dances. Today, we still wear masks for fun and at parties.

The masks in this book are easy to make from everyday things you can usually find at home or school. Ask an adult to help you get the things together. Make sure you look through each project carefully before you start making a mask.

Ask an adult to help you when you need to cut things. You'll be using a knife or a hole punch to make holes for your eyes to look through. Holes for eyes should be about ½cm wide and about 7cm apart.

Every mask is simply a beginning. You can add more textures, patterns and colours. Add as many as you wish. Your masks don't have to look like ours - they will be much more fun if they don't!

Masks by Geoff Redmayne.

Painted faces

The simplest mask of all is a painted face.

People paint their faces for many different reasons such as religious festivals, carnivals, camouflage or just for fun. We are going to make a clown face.

You will need:
A mirror
Non-toxic face paints
Brightly coloured, thick
  wool
Scissors
Rubber band

Look in the mirror and pull some funny faces. What happens to your mouth if you look sad?

With your face paints, and looking in your mirror, draw a short line going straight up above each eye. Then draw another line down below each eye. Be careful not to get paint in your eyes.

6

Now draw lines from your eye corners.
Move your eyes from side to side.

Paint your face in different ways. Paint
your lips bigger than they are. Paint the
lines and shapes in your face, like the
curve of your eyebrows or the shape of
your cheeks.

See how different colours make your
face look. Try light and dark colours.

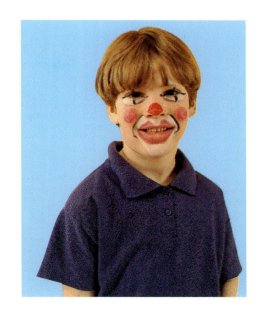

Add a mop of hair.
Cut lots of wool into
60cm lengths. Lay the
strands together and
tie them with a rubber
band in the middle.
Put the wool on your
head, with the strands
falling down around
your face.

Picture glasses

Look at your family, friends and other people around you. Everyone's face is different. There are always lots of photographs of different faces in magazines.

You will need:

Old magazines

Scissors

Card

Pencil

Glue

Felt-tipped pens or paints

Hole punch

Look through magazines and cut out some big eyes. You can use these to make a pair of glasses.

● Take a large piece of card. Draw the shape of a pair of glasses with arms that will bend back and sit over your ears. You could draw carefully around a pair of glasses first to give the sort of shape you need.

- Cut out your glasses from the card.
- Stick some big eyes behind the frames of your glasses, so that they can be seen from the front.
- Make small holes in the centre of the eyes so that you can see through them.
- Now, bend the arms back and put your glasses on.

You can add patterns and colours with felt-tipped pens or paints. Make your glasses as big and as funny as you like. You could add a nose and mouth, too.

9

Mosaic faces

A long time ago, artists made pictures and patterns like this on floors and walls. They used small pieces of coloured stone which they stuck down. This is called mosaic.

You will need:

Card or a plain paper plate

Old magazines

Scissors

Pencil

Glue

Hole punch or knife

Elastic

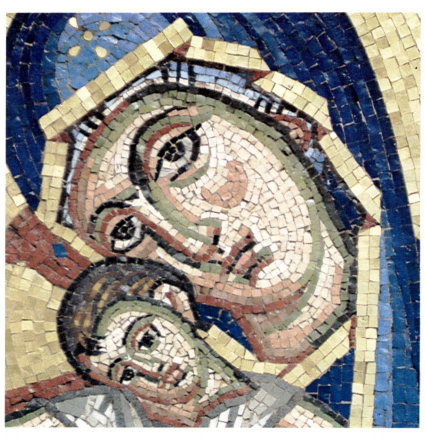

Mosaic faces of Mary with baby Jesus, from the Kykko monastery in Cyprus.

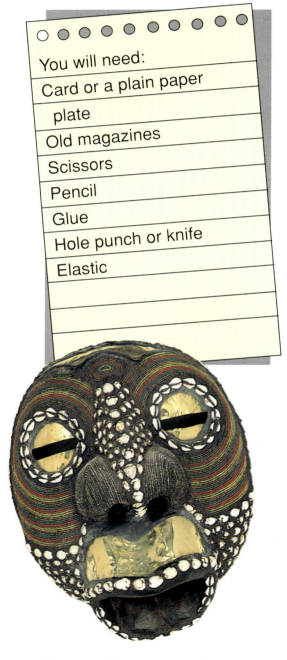

Eastern Nigerian mask decorated with beads and shells.

You can make a mosaic mask. Think about the colours you want to use for your mosaic mask. Tear or cut out different colours from magazines. You could collect skin colours, very bright colours, or different parts of faces like noses, eyes, and mouths.

- Take a paper plate or draw and cut out a face shape about 22cm long by 18cm wide from card.
- Draw lightly on your shape where you want the eyes, nose and mouth to be.
- Stick small pieces of magazine on to your mask to make a lively, colourful face.
- Make holes for your eyes to see through.

- Make a small hole on each side of your mask, in line with the eyes.
- Push one end of the elastic through one hole from the back of the mask to the front. Make a knot in the end of the elastic at the front of the mask, so that it cannot pull through the hole.
- Do the same with the other end of the elastic on the other side of the mask.

Cartoon characters

Look at these children's drawings of cartoon characters. What makes each character look different from any other? One might wear a special hat. Another might have a round nose or funny hair.

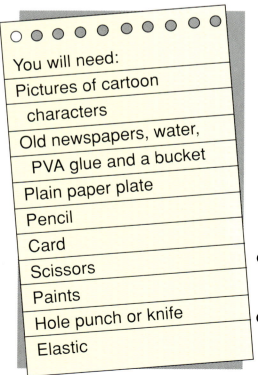

You will need:

Pictures of cartoon characters

Old newspapers, water, PVA glue and a bucket

Plain paper plate

Pencil

Card

Scissors

Paints

Hole punch or knife

Elastic

Let's make a mask of your favourite cartoon character. So far in this book you have made masks that are flat. Now build up the shape of a face using card or papier mâché, a sort of mushy paper.

Papier mâché is made like this (ask an adult to help you):

● Tear up some old newspaper into lots of small squares.
● Put the newspaper pieces into a bucket and cover with warm water.

- Leave the bucket like this until the next day. Then, carefully pour the water out, leaving the wet newspaper behind.
- Using your hands, mix enough PVA glue into the wet newspaper to make it soft and sticky.

Now make your mask.

- Draw the face of your character on a paper plate. Make holes for your eyes.
- You can add things like hats by sticking on extra pieces of card.

- Build up the shapes of cheeks, eyebrows and nose by adding more pieces of card and wet papier mâché pulp.
- When your mask is dry, paint it to look like your cartoon character. To wear your mask, add elastic as you did on page 11.

13

Self-portraits

We all look different because our faces are different shapes and colours.

You will need:

A blown-up balloon

Old newspapers

Wallpaper paste and brush

Pin

Hole punch and knife

Pencil

Mirror

Papier mâché pulp
  (see page 12)

Paints

Elastic

With this mask you make your own face. It is called a self-portrait.

Faces are not flat. They are rounded. That is why you start to make this mask on a blown-up balloon. This project uses another method of papier mâché called layering.

- Tear up some old newspaper into lots of small pieces.
- Ask an adult to help you mix up some wallpaper paste.
- Brush each side of the newspaper pieces with plenty of paste and cover the balloon with four layers.

- When the newspaper is dry, pop the balloon with a pin.
- Ask an adult to help you cut your newspaper balloon in half with a knife. Now you have the start of two masks.
- Draw where you want the eyes, nose and mouth to be, and cut holes for your eyes.

  Look at your face in a mirror. Which parts of your face stick out, or are curved or flat?

- Now build up your face on your mask with papier mâché, just like the last project.

When you have finished, leave your self-portrait to dry. Then paint it, looking at all the different colours in your face. Add elastic (see page 11) so that you can wear it.

Modelling with dough

Some masks are made by cutting the shapes and lines out of wood. Many masks are made by modelling something when it is soft, like clay or papier mâché, then drying it till it is hard.

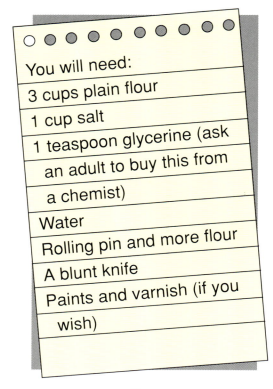

You will need:

3 cups plain flour

1 cup salt

1 teaspoon glycerine (ask an adult to buy this from a chemist)

Water

Rolling pin and more flour

A blunt knife

Paints and varnish (if you wish)

A Tlingit tribal mask of wood, fibre and feathers, North West American Coast.

You can also model a mask using soft bread dough. Ask an adult to help you.

- Make the dough in a bowl. Mix together the flour, salt and glycerine with about 1½ cups of water. The mixture should become like soft Plasticine.
- Press out some dough, about 1cm thick, on a flat work top. Make a big face shape. (Cover the work top with flour so that your dough does not stick.)
- Now make the shapes of a face in the dough.

You can use a blunt knife to make lines. Model shapes by squeezing and pulling the dough with your fingers. Ask an adult to help you bake your mask. Put it in a warm oven at 130°C for about 1 to 1½ hours until it is dry, but not brown. When your mask is dry, you can paint it. Varnish will make the mask very shiny.

Add all sorts of other things to make your mask exciting. Stick on feathers, shells or beads, make holes in the mask and push string, wool or rags through. Hang up your finished mask.

Animals

Animal faces make wonderful masks. Look at pictures of animals. Think of all the different masks you could make. You can make masks of real animals or think up your own wild creatures.

You will need:

An empty cereal packet

Pencil

Scissors

Glue

Paints

A variety of things to stick on your masks, such as feathers, wool and fabric

Hole punch or knife

Elastic

● Take the back of a cereal packet. Ask an adult to help you copy the lines from the picture below on to your piece of card. The dotted lines are where you will fold the card. Cut along the blue lines.

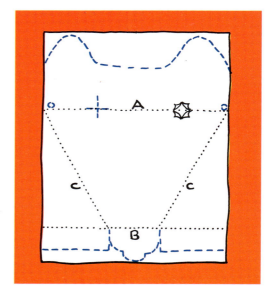

18

- Make the eyes by cutting two crosses like those in the picture. Then fold out each of the four points.
- Now fold the top part of the card along line 'A' so that it sticks up.
- Fold the bottom part of the card along line 'B' so that it points down.
- Fold the sides downwards along the lines marked 'C' to make a long nose. Stick the flaps of card under the end of the nose with some glue.

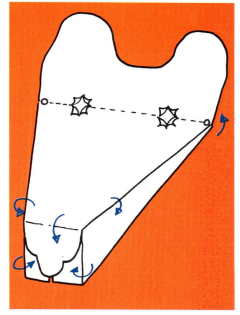

Use paints or collect things like feathers, string, strips of coloured paper, fabric and wool to make interesting animal markings.

Add some elastic, as you did on page 11, and put on your mask.

Pecking birds

You will need:

An empty cereal packet

Pencil

Ruler

Scissors or knife

Glue

Split pins

Paints or coloured papers

Green garden stick

Coloured feathers

Elastic

American Indians used to make bird masks which they held up on sticks when they danced. They could also make the bird's beak move.

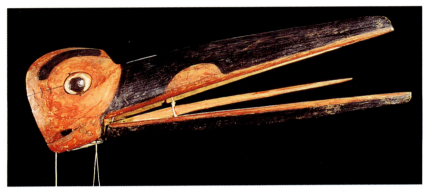

Nishga bird mask, North West American Coast.

Ask an adult to help you make a bird mask with a beak that moves. Look at the diagrams carefully.

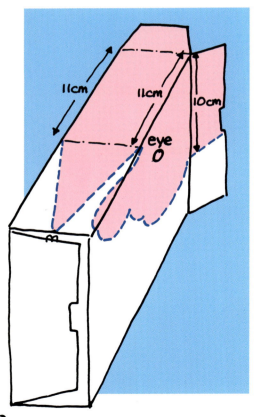

- You will use all of your cereal packet.
- Measure down 11cm at each corner of one long, narrow side. Make a mark at the middle of the bottom edge (m), and draw lines to the 11cm marks to make a 'V'-shaped tongue.
- Now draw your bird's head shape on both sides of the box (copy this from the picture on the left). Cut out the head and tongue (the shaded area). Make an eyehole on either side.

- Now take the rest of the box and flatten it out. Measure out the width of the side panel (x) along the top of the front (A) and at the bottom of the back (B). Now draw lines as shown in the picture. Cut out the beaks by following these blue lines.
- Stick the upper beak above the 'V'-shaped tongue on your mask.
- Slide the lower beak in under the tongue and attach with split pins. Glue on a stick to make your beak open and close.

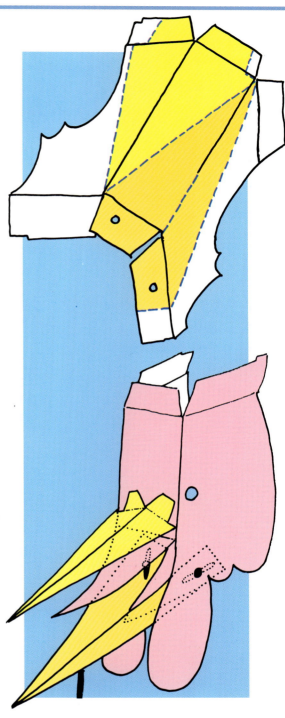

Glue or paint brightly coloured feathers on to your mask. Add some elastic (see page 11).

Hiding in the rainforest

Look at this painting of animals in a rainforest. Some of the animals are hiding behind the trees and leafy plants.

Part of *The Dream* by Henri Rousseau (1844-1910).

You can make a mask which hides behind another mask using a whole cereal packet.

- Draw and paint big leaf shapes filling the front of the cereal packet.
- Cut out to make two 'doors' as shown. This is the 'front' mask which hides another mask behind it.
- Open the doors. On the back of the packet draw and make an animal mask like you did before (see pages 18-19). Add elastic as you did on page 11.
- Go back to the 'front' mask. Glue the top of a stick to each door.

When you put on your mask, you can use the sticks to open the doors and show the animal behind.

This picture shows a mask of a bird hiding a mask of a man's face. It is an old North American Indian mask and was worn in tribal dances. You could make a mask like this, or you could make a mask of one happy and one sad face.

Tribal mask, North West American Coast

Try out your own ideas. You can add papier mâché (see page 12) or stick things on to add different textures.

23

Wild beasts

You will need:

Card or a plain paper
plate

Scissors

A variety of things you
can find to make an
unusual mask

Glue

Paints

Hole punch or knife

Elastic

Masks can be made from almost anything. This picture shows what one artist did with an old bicycle seat and some handlebars.

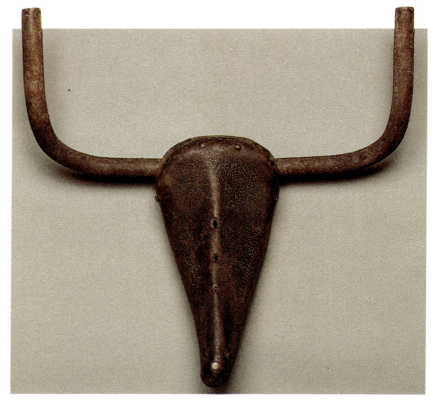

Bull's Head 1942 by Pablo Picasso (1881-1973).

Collect together lots of things you could use to make an interesting mask. Look around your home. Then see what else you can find outside. Collect all sorts of things like cardboard tubes, empty yoghurt pots, egg boxes, corrugated card, bottle tops, tree bark, sticks, feathers and dried leaves.

Look at all your finds and think about what sort of mask you are going to make with them.

- Use a paper plate as your mask shape or cut a big face shape out of card.
- Now add your found objects, sticking them on with glue. Make interesting textures and patterns. Keep sticking things down until you have something really wild and exciting. Use your paints, as well.

If your mask is not too heavy to wear, make holes for your eyes and add some elastic as you did on page 11. If it is heavy, hang it on the wall instead. It will look just as good.

When you have been making masks in this book, you have been looking at faces from the front so that you see the whole face. What does a face look like from the side? The shape of a face when it is seen from the side is called a profile.

You will need:

Card

Pencil

Scissors

Glue

Hole punch

Paints

Elastic

Portrait of Dora Maar by Pablo Picasso (1881-1973).

Look at this painting. Can you see a picture of a face seen from the front as well as from the side?

Now make a mask like this.

● On one piece of card draw a whole face from the front. Draw a friend or a member of your family. Make it big.

- On another piece of card draw the same person's face from the side. Look carefully at the person's profile. You can see only one eye. What does it look like?
- Cut out both faces, and cut away the back of the head on the profile drawing. Now place the profile on top of the other face and move them around until you like the way they look. Then stick them together.

- Paint your mask brightly.
- Make holes for your eyes to look through, and add elastic (see page 11).

Chinese dragons

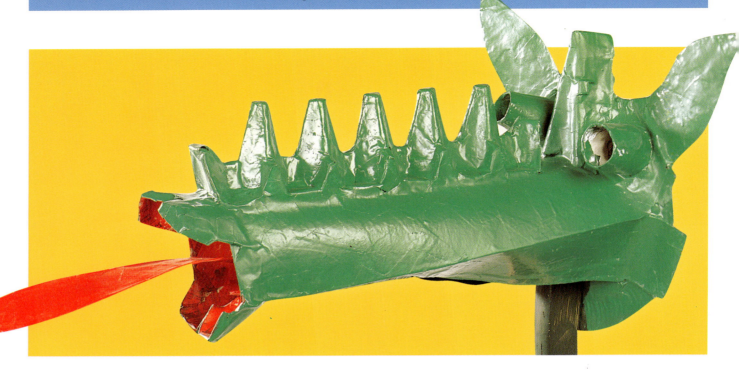

You will need:

A plain paper plate

Card

Pencil

Scissors

Glue

Paints

A variety of things you can find to make interesting masks, such as egg boxes, cereal packets, pieces of fabric and wool, silver foil

An old sheet (ask an adult for this)

This dragon's head was made with egg boxes, a cereal packet, a paper plate and some card.

Make up your own ideas for masks. Look around you and at pictures in books and magazines. Almost anything can be the beginning for a really exciting mask.

Think what things you can find to use. Everyday objects look very different when they have been painted or have had things added.

This colourful dragon twists and turns through the streets during Chinese New Year celebrations.

Get together with some friends and make a giant creature mask. You can use some of the ideas in this book to help.

Chinese New Year, London UK.

Ask an adult if there is an old sheet you can use. Paint the sheet or add pieces of fabric and other things to make the creature's body. One of you wears the mask while the others stand behind in a row and wriggle around like a monster's tail.

29

FIRST ARTS & CRAFTS: MASKS introduces young children to a wide variety of mask-making techniques and ideas. Whilst most of the masks are very simple to create, a few projects will require some adult help but give children a wider perspective on the potential of the craft. All the masks are made from easily found materials, most of which are everyday household items. Each project is clearly described and accompanied by a list of the required materials. Children should be encouraged to go through each project before they start, to ensure they have gathered all the materials. They should think in terms of the masks featured as pictures to inspire their own ideas. They can make the masks simple, or can add more and more texture, form, colour and pattern almost indefinitely.

Make sure scissors are safe for children to use, and encourage them to ask for adult help when things need cutting with a knife or hole punch.

Masks offer a wealth of opportunity for extension work and cross-curricular activities. Apart from the more obvious choices such as studies of tribal cultures, festivals across the world, animal markings and camouflage, acting and the theatre, you will find the projects inspire many other ideas. There are so many masks to stimulate the imagination that it is hard to make any recommendations. However, those of the American Indians are very good sources of ideas for materials, designs and added textures.

Listed below are any practical points or extension work that is relevant to particular chapters. Many of the ideas overlap and can be used in other projects throughout the book.

Making masks 4-5
A great deal has been written about masks, their supernatural powers and their links with ethnic cultures past and present. A good basic guide is *The Letts Guide to Collecting Masks* by Timothy Teuten (Charles Letts and Company Limited, 1991).

Painted faces 6-7
Encourage children to explore facial expressions in the mirror. They can try to recreate particular expressions by accentuating the lines of their faces with their face paints. Use pictures to introduce them to tribal and ritual face painting. They can also explore painting themselves as animals.

Mosaic masks 10-11
There are many fine examples of mosaic for children to look at and learn about either in books or on field trips. The project can also be linked to the collage techniques of another book in this series, *First Arts & Crafts: Collage*, and, of course, to the work of Picasso and the Cubists. Encourage children to look for the different colours in faces. However, the masks they make need not be realistic. Indeed, encourage imaginative approaches such as using bright colours or different shades of one colour and so on.

Self-portraits 14-15

Again, children should look closely at, in this case, the different colours in their own faces using a mirror. Ask them to compare their own faces with those of friends and family, looking at the shapes of features as well as colour. An amusing extension of this project is to make a self-portrait with features which are much larger than they really are.

Modelling with dough 16-17

Look at masks from different countries, especially Africa. This project also provides a useful link to looking at sculpture, both contemporary and historical. Much classical sculpture is superbly modelled and of beautiful simplicity and proportion. The twentieth century, with such sculptors as Rodin, Epstein and Frink, offers a rich source. Encourage children to think about form and proportion by looking and feeling. When using the dough, children can build up parts of the mask while it is still soft by pressing on other pieces of soft dough which have been wet with a little water first.

Animals 18-19

To make folding the card easier, use the back of a pair of scissors to score down the fold lines first. The animal masks can be built up with papier mache if wished. A group of children could make a number of different farm animals and act out *Old MacDonald*.

Wild beasts 24-25

As they gather materials together, children should be encouraged to think about the differences between man-made and natural forms. Feeling and responding to textures is important, as is the ability to see that something can become something else. This links, again, with materials used in collage.

Front and side 26-27

The simplicity and apparent crudity of the work of Picasso, its strong colour, inventiveness and use of materials, are a tremendous source of ideas for children. Using a strong light to project profiles onto a wall can be useful and fun. The profile can also be seen in Renaissance portraiture and, of course, in early Egyptian tomb paintings, these showing the traditions from which modern art has been developed.

Further information

Glossary

Actor A person who pretends to be someone or something else in a play.

Camouflage A colour or pattern which matches the surroundings. A camouflaged person or animal is difficult to see.

Cave people People who lived in caves a long, long time ago.

Crops Plants which are grown by people, usually to eat.

Elastic A stretchy thread.

Festivals Special days or times of the year during which people celebrate something.

Glycerine A thick, clear, sweet liquid.

Hole punch A special tool for making different sized holes.

Modelling Shaping something out of a soft material, like clay or Plasticine.

Mysterious Something secret.

Non-toxic Not poisonous.

Pair Two things which go together.

Profile The shape of a face seen from the side.

PVA glue A water based glue.

Self-portrait A picture of oneself.

Split pins Pins with two ends. When the pin is pushed through something, the two ends are bent backwards to hold the pin in place.

Texture The feel or look of a surface.

Index

Acknowledgements

The publishers wish to thank the following for the use of photographs:
Robert Harding Picture Library for p.4 Tassili rock painting, Algeria © F. Jackson and p.29 Chinese New Year, London UK © Adam Woolfit.
Eye Ubiquitous for p.5 Masks © Geoff Redmayne; p.6 (top left) Aborigine from Kakadu, Australia © Matthew McKee and p.6 (top middle) Chinese opera performer © Julia Waterlow.
Reproduced by kind permission of Christie's Images, p.16 Tlingit tribal mask.
© The British Museum, London for p.20 Nishga bird mask and p.23 Tribal mask.
The Bridgeman Art Library, London for p.22 *The Dream*, Henri Rousseau © Museum of Modern Art, New York and p.26 *Portrait of Dora Maar* by Pablo Picasso © DACS 1994.
Musée Picasso, Paris for p.24 *Bulls Head 1942* by Pablo Picasso © DACS 1994.
Badger p.18 by Bridget Sherlock.
All other photographs © Chris Fairclough Colour Library.

The publishers also wish to thank our models Jack, Sophie, Manlai and Kerry, and our young artists Harry, Sophie and Jack.